D1556230

# CHAIN OF EVIDENCE

# Workbook

Timothy Sweetman

Adele Sweetman

WADSWORTH
CENGAGE Learning

Australia • Brazil • Japan • Korea • Mexico • Singapore • Spain • United Kingdom • United States

**Chain of Evidence Workbook**
Timothy Sweetman, Adele Sweetman

For product information and technology assistance, contact us at
**Cengage Learning Customer & Sales Support, 1-800-354-9706**

For permission to use material from this text or product, submit all requests online at **cengage.com/permissions**
Further permissions questions can be emailed to
**permissionrequest@cengage.com**

Library of Congress Catalog Number: 98-70364

ISBN-13: 978-0-942728-86-6

ISBN-10: 0-942728-86-6

**Wadsworth**
10 Davis Drive
Belmont, CA 94002-3098
USA

Cengage Learning is a leading provider of customized learning solutions with office locations around the globe, including Singapore, the United Kingdom, Australia, Mexico, Brazil, and Japan. Locate your local office at: **international.cengage.com/region**

Cengage Learning products are represented in Canada by Nelson Education, Ltd.

For your course and learning solutions, visit **academic.cengage.com**

Purchase any of our products at your local college store or at our preferred online store **www.ichapters.com**

Printed in the United States of America
7 8 9 10 11 10

# Dedication

For Kathleen, Jack, Artie, Edmund, Lisa Ayn, Sean, Krystal and Thomas-Christopher, with love

# Acknowledgment

Our special thanks to Sergeant Tom Delgado, supervisor of a Robbery/Homicide unit and an experienced homicide detective, for his valuable factual contribution.

**Chain of Custody.** In evidence, the one who offers real evidence, such as the narcotics in a trial of a drug case, must account for the custody of the evidence from the moment in which it reaches his custody until the moment in which it is offered in evidence, and such evidence goes to weight not to admissibility of evidence.

*Black's Law Dictionary, 6th Edition*

## Declaration

The persons portrayed in this text are actual people, some living, some dead. However, to protect their privacy, the names of these individuals have been changed.

# Contents

## To Students

Chain of custody, it is said, successfully occurs when someone such as you, the detective, testifies under oath that you identified, took control of an item of real evidence and placed it into storage or released it to an expert, such as a toxicologist, to be further analyzed. Then, the day of trial you retrieved the item to be offered into court as evidence.

The evidence, having passed through the proper linking procedure appears secure. But is it? Not always. Why? Lack of communication and error. Communication, as you will learn from your forthcoming investigation, though incidental to the chain of custody, must coat every link of the chain, or the process of documenting custody (from this hand to that hand) will be merely chain-like and, thus, not convincing.

Indeed, failure to pass the collected evidence through its proper channels can render the process void and, similarly, a break in communication can weaken the chain of custody and render the process disputable. The consequences? Your open/shut case against the suspect(s) is substantially weakened.

For example, Suzanne Temple murders her husband, Alex Temple. She spices up his red chile burrito—his last burrito—with a dose of potassium cyanide, ambushes him with a loaded gun as he sits quietly at his computer, scripts a "Damsel in Distress" melodrama, then fabricates the burglary/murder scenario. Her punishment? A possible first degree murder melts the ruling down to a second degree, then to voluntary manslaughter. Why? Because the chain of custody did not hold up the links. Unfortunately, they were neither coated with good communication nor with precaution against error.

*Tim Sweetman*

*Adele Sweetman*

# About the Authors

Tim Sweetman spent 13 years in law enforcement. He worked patrol, community relations, street gang and narcotics before spending three years as a homicide detective and a year as a homicide sergeant. Currently, he is a full-time administration of justice professor at Los Angeles City College, Los Angeles, California. He earned a Master of Arts degree in Public Administration at California State University, Northridge, a Bachelor of Science degree in Marketing from California State Polytechnic University, Pomona and an Associate of Arts degree in Administration of Justice at Pasadena City College.

Adele Sweetman writes True-Crime. She is also a full-time General Education professor at Mt. Sierra College in Monrovia, California and a part-time English professor at DeVry Institute of Technology in Pomona, California. She earned her Master of Arts degree in creative writing at California State University, Northridge, a Bachelor of Arts degree in English at California State Polytechnic University, Pomona and an American Bar Association Certified Litigation Legal Assistant Specialist degree at California State University, Los Angeles.

*Chapter 1*

# Who, What, When, Where, Why and How

It's the 14th day of September. At 10:30 p.m. you learn that Alex Temple is dead. He was shot to death in his home. Seconds after hanging up the telephone, you are showering, your thoughts replaying the conversation you just had with the WATCH COMMANDER, your mind organizing the scant amount of information. You get dressed, slip into your shoes and race out the door, a cup of coffee in your hand. You're all set for the long night ahead. Already, you have determined that maybe, if you're lucky, certain evidence directly related to the crime will be on the premises—evidence you can piece together to learn why and how the murder occurred.

It is your understanding that his wife, Suzanne Temple, called the 911 operator and asked that they send the paramedics to her home. According to the operator, she was sobbing, "He was just lying here, bleeding all over when I returned from the bowling alley." She had only been gone a few hours. You are also told that Temple told the operator that "I don't think he's breathing," and you wonder why Temple didn't ask that police be sent as well.

You are the assigned lead detective. It's your job to make sure that the investigation is conducted properly, that evidence is correctly preserved and that witnesses are identified. Indeed, it is your job to find out who killed Alex Temple so that the murderer is held accountable.

Most deaths, like most births, occur after sunset. This death is no exception. Generally, the high beams of your detective unit, a white Chevy Lumina, shine ahead to help you and your partner locate addresses. On this night, however, it isn't necessary. You are familiar with the streets' grid in this northeast area. Besides, several police cars are parked in front of 1114 Brickman Road and, as usual, more than a dozen curious on-lookers already surround townhouse #5—your destination.

Already, at midnight, the time you arrive at the crime scene, the FIRST OF-FICER at the SCENE (FOS) has contacted the neighbor who called the police department and identified the witnesses at the crime scene. Also, upon seeing a "man down" the OFFICER called for assistance.

In the meantime, the FOS conducted a visual search of the townhouse for other victims and visible evidence. He knew that the Emergency Doctrine protects him against improper search and seizure allegations; it allows for a warrantless search and seizure when there is probable cause to believe a life-threatening situation exists and there is no time to secure a search warrant.

Minutes later, when a SECOND and THIRD OFFICER arrived, followed by the SUPERVISOR, coordination of priorities began. The SUPERVISOR confirmed that a homicide did, indeed, occur, then notified the WATCH COMMANDER who called the DETECTIVES. The FOS directed the SECOND OFFICER to seal off the crime scene area with yellow police tape. "Freezing" (sealing off) the homicide scene is the best way to preserve the evidence.

Once the crime scene was secured, a THIRD OFFICER was posted at the door of the townhouse to log in the names and times of those coming and going, and to aggressively keep "looky loo" police officers at bay. These precautions were taken to reduce the possibility of contaminating evidence. Inevitably, some officers and, in high profile cases, some administrators go into crime scenes for curiosity sake without realizing that they can contaminate potential evidence by stepping on it, touching it, or just by their very presence can create chaos at a time when order is essential. The most important part of a crime scene investigation is to identify the evidence, preserve it and collect it properly to ensure accurate analysis.

Upon your arrival, you make contact with the FOS but your attention is drawn to a slim, striking female in her late twenties. She's slumped over on the living room sofa, the palms of her hands anchored around long, extended legs. Her sandy hair, silky and below the shoulders, hides her face. The FOS detects your curiosity and introduces you to Suzanne Temple, the victim's wife. Her brown almond-shaped eyes are red and swollen, but she manages a smile. A FRIEND from a neighboring townhouse is beside her offering support. Off to the side, the OFFICER briefs you as to what he did and what evidence he saw during the visual search. With the OFFICER'S information in mind, you begin a walk-through to see for yourself what evidence will be available to assist your investigation.

In the living room, you notice a Dodger's baseball cap next to the front door. The cap appears to have a hole on its right side and fresh blood on the rear adjustable plastic tab. To your left, on the north wall of the living room, is a window. The outside window screen has been removed; it is inside the townhouse leaning against a white loveseat.

Alex Temple is at the foot of the stairway near the dining room. He is lying on his right side, his head turned to his right, his brown eyes half open, brown curly hair stained with blood. His profile carves a strong nose and full mouth. A blood-soaked towel and lead projectile lie on the beige carpeted floor next to the victim. He is clothed in shorts; his wallet protrudes from a back pocket, a few credit cards scattered alongside his tan, muscular calves.

Outside, south of the dining room, is a patio; you notice the glass sliding door is partly open.

Upstairs, in what appears to be a workroom, you notice blood spatter on a chair and on the cover of a *Time* magazine lying on the floor.

A kingsize waterbed in the master bedroom occupies most of the available space. It is unmade. The blanket and white goose down comforter are partially off the sides of the bed. A six-drawer dresser is at the foot of the bed. Three things catch your eye: (1) an ammunition box—nearly full—on top of the dresser, (2) most of the drawers are partially open and, (3) clothes inside are strewn upside down. It appears to you that the room could have been ransacked.

On your return to the lower level, you notice a dried, bloody fingerprint on a wall and blood spatter on the staircase railing.

You have noted your findings for the eventual crime scene search.

More pressing now are the witnesses. They are waiting to speak to you. The young grieving widow is still sitting in the living room whimpering; her nose has reddened and crocodile tears stain her cheeks. You decide to interview her later at the station. You ask that an officer transport her to the police station, then you excuse Temple's friend.

It's time to look for the other witnesses identified earlier by the FOS. You knock on each door respectively, introduce yourself, and pull out your yellow notepad. The Temple's solicitous neighbors remember much about this particular evening and *much* of what they recall looks to be relevant.

A NEIGHBOR, his GIRLFRIEND and her TEENAGE DAUGHTER, who share a common wall with the Temples, and the MANAGER who manages the townhouse complex, tell you what they heard and saw. Each corroborates all or part of the other's information.

The NEIGHBOR and GIRLFRIEND tell you that about 9:00 p.m., they were relaxing in their patio, both on their second cigarette, when they heard four consecutive shots, followed by a woman's scream. Both believe the shots originated in the townhouse next door. Admittedly, they were shaken because earlier, while the three were having dinner, they heard the residents yelling. This was unusual because they were rarely heard arguing; they appeared to be "happy" and seemingly "did everything together." Attempts to eavesdrop were futile. The voices were muffled but the yelling was loud enough to be heard over the *Wonder Years* program that had been left on in the living room.

After the shots sounded, the TEENAGER was their first concern and both ran into the living room to check on her. The fifteen-year-old was on the telephone, the program *Beverly Hills 90210* blasting. Nonetheless, she, too, heard several gun shots that seemed to come from the "other side of the wall." She also heard a "loud scream" and what sounded like "something tumbling down a staircase." At first, the three contemplated calling the police, then decided, instead, to notify the MANAGER.

They say the following happened: Suzanne Temple was locking the front door when they approached her. She turned and asked the witnesses, "What's up?" She appeared nervous and upset but unconcerned. "I didn't hear anything. I'm alright. Everything's fine. I hear shots down here all the time. Yeah, once I heard gunshots from another city. Hey, I gotta go bowling."

Three of the witnesses agree that Suzanne was wearing a light-colored shirt and dark shorts. They say she clutched a dark brown purse with a long strap to her chest with her right hand.

The TEENAGER remembers more. From her angle, a left side angle, she saw some kind of white tissue with some dark spots, "maybe like blood," dangling from between Suzanne's thumb and index finger. This was visible even though she held the purse tightly over the hand with the tissue.

Moreover, the TEENAGER, a "clothes freak," remembers exactly what the lady wore: ivy green shorts, dark blue long sleeve sweater with something white, possibly a Peter Pan collar, coming out of the neck.

They say that when Suzanne excused herself and went to her car, they each returned to their homes. The MANAGER had had no problem with Suzanne's explanation; however, the neighbors had not been convinced.

Their suspicions were confirmed at about 10:30 p.m. that same evening. Through the thin plaster board walls, they heard more commotion in the neighboring townhouse: running up the stairs, running down the stairs, screaming. Seconds later there was a loud knock on their front door. It was Suzanne Temple. She "kind of collapsed against the front door" and pleaded, "somebody help me. My husband is hurt. Somebody is on the phone."

The NEIGHBOR states that he reiterated his earlier gut feeling. "Ha! So those were shots we heard earlier."

This time Mrs. Temple conceded, "Yes, they were shots."

In the townhouse, the NEIGHBOR found Mr. Temple lying on the floor at the base of the staircase. A 911 operator was on the phone, but before the operator could instruct CPR, the paramedics arrived. It was too late. Alex Temple was dead.

Name _____          Date _____

# QUESTIONS - CHAPTER ONE

1.  Before you arrive at the crime scene, you speculate as to what may have lead to the death of Alex Temple. Sort out some common scenarios.

2.  Based on what you know, what kind of real evidence might you expect to find at the crime scene?

3.  The blood spatter evidence helps determine the physical movements of the person(s) involved in Alex Temple's death. What is your interpretation of this evidence?

Name _____          Date _____

**QUESTIONS - CHAPTER 1 CONTINUED**

4.  The bloody fingerprint in the hallway is potentially your best evidence at the scene. Why?

5.  Why do you interview the neighbors before you search the crime scene in depth?

Name _____          Date _____

## QUESTIONS - CHAPTER 1 CONTINUED

6.  What potential piece of evidence did the neighbor's TEENAGE DAUGHTER see Suzanne Temple holding? Why is this important?

7.  Who is your prime suspect at this time? Explain.

# Chapter 2

# The Townhouse

The townhouse, you notice, looks lived-in and homey, containing a cozy bean bag, stained wood crate, cat tree, Dodger-Blue paraphernalia, stationary exercise bicycle, weight bench, a Schwinn ten speed, etc.

Structurally, however, the townhouse is typical of many other such living quarters. Downstairs is the living room, dining room, kitchen and bathroom. Upstairs is the master bedroom, bedroom/office and bathroom. Stairs connect the lower and upper levels.

Is a search warrant needed?

Anytime a homicide victim is found in a residence a search warrant is needed. Police cannot discount that those who live at the residence are possible suspects, and because they have "standing" to their property—the right to challenge a search if done without consent or a warrant—a search warrant is a must.

Your search warrant has been signed by a JUDGE. It indicates that there is probable cause to believe that property "used as a means of committing a felony and tending to show that a felony has been committed or that a particular person has committed a felony" may be found in the townhouse and vehicles at the location. Accordingly, the following property is "lawfully seizable":

1.  Any firearm for comparison to the projectiles in or around the victim.

2.  Any and all ammunition.

3.  Any blood or blood stained items.

4.  Any documents or photographs showing an association to Alex Temple.

5.  Any information in the computer that may have been entered by the victim about the possible attack on his life.

6.  A 1988 red Dodge truck with a shell, license 3ST3073, registered to Alex Temple.

7.  A 1993 red Infiniti, license 8LAT768, registered to Suzanne Temple.

8.  Any personal property that tends to show or establish the identity of the persons in "control of the residence."

YOU and your PARTNER are ready to search the townhouse and vehicles for evidence.

In the living room is one recoverable item—the bloody baseball cap that you saw earlier along the west wall.

> Bloody items taken as evidence must first be air dried. Packaging wet blood may lead to contamination. Therefore, prior to packaging the baseball cap, the blood must be completely dry. The item is then packaged in paper; using plastic may lead to contamination. Also, the cap must be packaged separately to avoid cross-contamination.

The outside living room window screen leaning against the north wall is not an issue. Suzanne's FRIEND explained earlier that the Temples had locked themselves out of the townhouse that week and that Alex climbed through the window to open the door. A closer look at the window revealed that it was locked from the inside. Even with this knowledge, you will still ask that the EVIDENCE TECHNICIANS dust the window and screen for fingerprints.

Five items in the dining room are recoverable. A white, bloody towel is by the victim's right hip. A cellular telephone is near his head. Several inches away from the victim's legs is an expended lead projectile. Also recoverable are the credit cards that lie scattered around the victim's buttocks. The victim is wearing a solid dark blue t-shirt, cutoff 501 Levis, white ankle socks and white Wilson tennis shoes. Near the left Levi pocket is a brown wallet that appears to have fallen out or have been taken out.

> The bloody towel must be dried before packaging it. The cellular telephone must be carefully handled so as not to compromise the fingerprint analysis. It is best to wear gloves. In addition, the cellular telephone should be inspected for a serial or identification number. This number, with a description of the phone, should be written on the outside of the evidence bag containing the phone. The lead projectile should be picked up by gloved fingers as well, not a metal object like tweezers or pliers. Metal objects will scratch the material and may contaminate the object and compromise the results. The credit cards and the wallet will be collected, then packaged separately. Careful handling with gloved hands is needed so that possible fingerprints are not disturbed. The cards cannot be returned to the wallet because there is a possibility of smudging any print on the card.

You notice the hot water is running in the kitchen sink at a small, but steady, pace. Next to the sink is a damp green dish towel with stains that you think could be blood. A container of Comet also has a stain on it. These items are recovered.

If possible, it is best to take the entire item that has blood on it, so the blood won't be disturbed. The EVIDENCE TECHNICIANS must package the green dish towel, as well as package the entire container of Comet, rather than cut out the blood stain.

The office on the second floor is the first accessible room from the stair landing. It's quite large. In it are several desks; business papers and computer programs clutter the formica tops. On a couple of desks sit computers. You notice one is turned on. A brown swivel arm chair sits back from the operating computer toward the middle of the room; blood spatter stains the back of the backrest and several blood droppings cling to the armrest. Just below the chair on the floor is a *Time* magazine; on its cover is a blood spot. You speculate that the victim may have been sitting in the chair when he was shot. You are not sure, at this time, how he ended up downstairs.

Some items may be too big or impractical to remove in order to preserve a drop or smear of blood. In these cases, the entire item should first be photographed. A second photograph focuses on the blood stain. The third photograph indicates the measurements of the stain. The stain should be photographed with an L-shaped ruler beside it to show the length. Experts can view these photographs and possibly determine the position of the body when it lost the blood. Lastly, the blood stain, once dried, can be chipped off with a razor. The dried blood is then packaged and placed into evidence. The magazine is taken and placed in evidence. The key to these particular pieces of evidence is their positioning (and form) to the chair. From this, blood spatter interpretation can be made. Therefore, a photograph is needed to show the positioning of the blood stain on the chair and the magazine in relation to each other.

The furniture in the master bedroom consists of a waterbed and a dresser. A circular white-gold diamond wedding band and matching diamond bracelet are on the dresser. An empty Taurus .38 caliber gun box and a box of .38 caliber bullets are also on the dresser. The gun box appears new, and when you count the rounds in the ammunition box, you learn that five rounds are missing. No gun is found.

The gun box and ammunition box must be carefully handled to preserve fingerprints. The bullets will be removed from the box, counted and packaged. The evidence custodian must be told beforehand that bullets are packaged in a certain envelope due to their potential danger.

In the shower of the upstairs bathroom hang a pair of female blue-jean shorts; they are damp, as if recently washed, but on the right rear pocket is a blood stain. Moreover, on the floor beside the toilet is a bloody bandage.

The blood stained shorts are handled like all bloody clothing. Allow the shorts and stain to completely dry. Photograph the item and package it in paper. The bloody bandage must also be fully dry. Photograph and package it separately from the shorts.

On your way downstairs, you take a second look at the bloody fingerprint on the waterheater cabinet door, located outside the office in the hallway.

A bloody fingerprint can be the most important evidence item in any homicide scene. If practical, remove the item that the print is on. In this case, remove the cabinet door and wrap it in paper so that the fingerprint technician and serologist can analyze it. When it is not practical to remove the item, the print has to be cut out of the item.

An enclosed outside patio is accessible through the sliding glass door at the south end of the dining room. The glass door is open about five inches. There is a bicycle leaning against the inside of that sliding glass door. About two inches more is all you can slide the door because the bicycle's wheels ground themselves securely into the carpet and the bicycle itself butts against the glass. A person of average size could not easily slide through the opening without knocking over the bicycle. Also, you notice that there are no signs of forced entry on the glass door. Checking further, you notice a large tree. The branches are hanging over the patio and the patio is carpeted with large maple leaves. None appear disturbed. There are no visible footprints.

The best way to preserve this scene is through photographs and videotape. Special attention should be given to the undisturbed ground, the interior and the exterior walls. Since an intruder may have left this bloody scene through the patio, blood evidence might be found on the leaves or patio perimeter dirt as well as blood stains on the wall where the suspect may have climbed over to flee. Even though there are no signs of forced entry, the glass door must be fingerprinted. If there are scratches on the lock, or if it doesn't work properly, the lock must be removed and analyzed for evidence of tampering.

The Infiniti, listed in your search warrant, is registered to Suzanne Temple. It's locked and parked in a stall. There are two bowling balls in cases on the passenger floorboard. The car appears clean except for a stain that could be blood on the driver's side electric seat adjuster. Several wet pieces of tissues are inside the open ashtray, and you think that these, too, might be suspect and worth collecting. (Later, you learn that she first drove the Infiniti, but on the freeway discovered her bowling equipment was in the other vehicle.)

If the seat adjuster can be removed, remove it. If not, allow the stain to fully dry and chip off the blood. Remember, a photograph is essential. The wet tissue should also be dried and packaged in paper. If the tissue smells of a chemical, package it in a plastic baggie, then place it in a paper bag.

The second vehicle, a red Dodge pickup truck, is registered to the victim. It is locked and parked at the rear of the townhouse. Inside the truckbed are four bowling balls each contained in a ball bag, as well as a handbag with miscellaneous bowling equipment. In the cab, you see a towel near the gas pedal. Under the driver's seat you find several white napkins with blood stains clumped together. The blood on the napkins appears fresh. (Later, you also learn that she ultimately drove the truck to the bowling alley.)

Bloody items that are clumped together should be packaged together; the evidence may be compromised if the paper towels are separated. Experts can tell if blood was deposited directly onto the paper towels or if the blood transfer was from tissue to tissue. If separated, this analysis would be more difficult.

Having completed the crime scene search, you direct the TECHNICIANS to number the evidence with blue placards and white numbering, photograph the evidence, sketch the scenes and recover the listed items.

The TECHNICIANS will recover all the items directed by you as well as other evidence they determine relevant. With that, the chain of custody will begin. The evidence must be marked or tagged, packaged and transported to the police station where it will be booked into evidence by the evidence/property custodian.

Property or evidence rooms are generic in appearance: usually large rooms, tiered shelves throughout and small walkways separating the shelves. The evidence custodian will place all the evidence items of a specified case in one area of a shelf. One exception are those evidence items that need to be refrigerated, like blood evidence. Another exception is an evidence item that is too large for the shelf. A secured "outside" evidence room is then used. The TECHNICIAN will remain at the scene to take other measurements and finish the sketches.

Meanwhile, you return to the police station to interview the victim's wife. From what you saw at the townhouse, it initially appeared that a burglary or robbery occurred. However, close inspection of the evidence and scene didn't add up to a burglary/robbery motive—it appeared manufactured. And, as a matter of course, when a spouse is murdered, the surviving spouse isn't quickly discounted as the suspect.

At the crime scene the CORONER INVESTIGATOR, using a gunshot residue kit (GSR), conducts a test on the victim's hands.

Typically, the CORONER INVESTIGATOR will conduct a GSR test on the victim. This is an investigative procedure that could establish if the victim had recently fired a gun or had his hands exposed to gunshot residue. The hands are sprayed with a chemical and then Q-tips are used to swab the areas of the hand. Each Q-tip is designated for a part of the hand, such as the right palm, the back of the right hand, etc. The Q-tips are packaged individually in small plastic tubes which are sealed by tape. The tubes are then placed in a paper GSR envelope. Even though the detective is accountable for this investigation, the GSR evidence will stay with the INVESTIGATOR, packaged and placed in the Coroner's evidence locker where it will stay pending analysis.

Thereafter, the INVESTIGATOR checks the victim for visible injuries. The victim has a bullet wound to his upper head, about the right ear. He has a through and through bullet wound to his left upper arm that appears to go from rear to front. There are two bullet wounds on the victims' back and both appear to be entry wounds. The INVESTIGATOR feels around and locates what seems to be a bullet just under the skin below an entry wound. No other signs of injury are found. The INVESTI-GATOR is of the opinion that the victim was shot five times.

Entrance wounds typically indent the skin and are slightly larger or smaller than the size of the bullet. At close range, bullet holes will be slightly larger because of the explosive gases. At longer distances, 18" or more, the gases dissipate into the atmosphere so wounds are slightly smaller. In addition, entrance wounds leave a gray ring around the wound because, as the bullet passes through the skin, residue is deposited onto the skin.

The INVESTIGATOR makes arrangements to have the body of Alex Temple taken to the coroner's office. The body is assigned case number 98-8166351.

Case number

Dining room and kitchen area

N

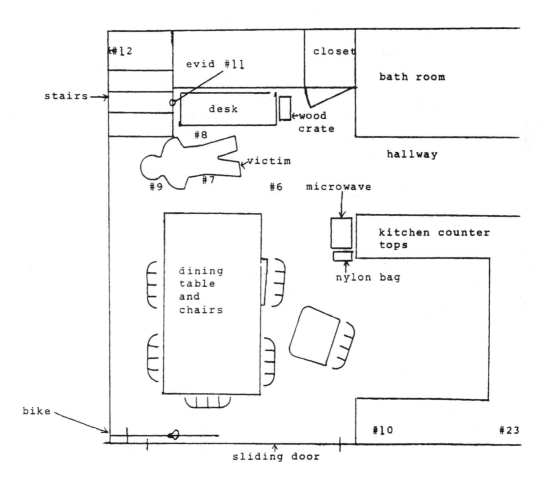

#12

evid #11

closet

bath room

stairs→

desk

←wood
crate

#8

hallway

victim

#9  #7  #6  microwave

nylon bag

dining
table
and
chairs

kitchen counter
tops

bike

#10  #23

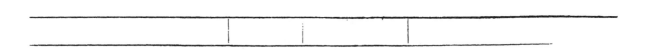
sliding door

| Date of this report | Case number |
| --- | --- |

2nd floor

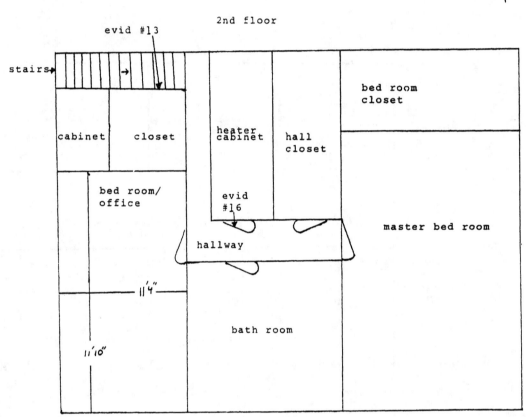

| Date of this report | Case number |
|---|---|

2nd floor bed room/office

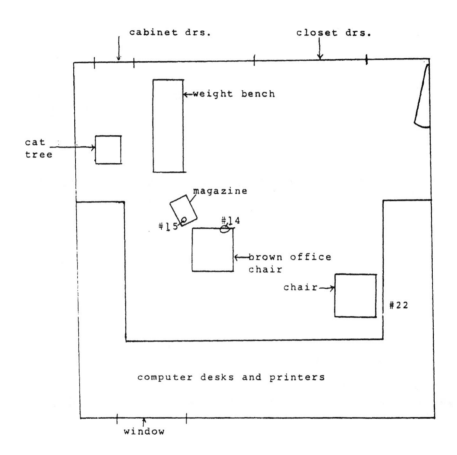

cabinet drs.          closet drs.

←weight bench

cat
tree →

magazine

#15      #14

←brown office
   chair

chair→   #22

computer desks and printers

↑
window

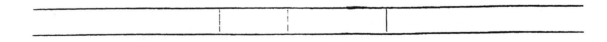

Name _____          Date _____

# QUESTIONS - CHAPTER TWO

1.  What initial steps are necessary in collecting real (physical) evidence that starts the chain of custody?

2.  What blood evidence items did you collect at the Temple's townhouse?

3.  What can you speculate, regarding the chain of events, as to the blood evidence?

Name _____        Date _____

## QUESTIONS - CHAPTER 2 CONTINUED

4.  What processing steps are needed to collect blood evidence?

    - From large objects?

    - From small objects?

5.  What is the possible significance in finding fresh blood evidence on tissues in the truck?

6.  What is your interpretation of the loose wallet and scattered credit cards near the body?

Name _____        Date _____

**QUESTIONS - CHAPTER 2 CONTINUED**

7.   What evidence, or lack of evidence, make you believe that the possible burglary/ robbery scenario was manufactured?

8.   What is the possible significance of the GSR evidence results from Alex Temple's hands?

# Chapter 3

# The Confession

It's well past midnight when you return to the police station to interrogate Suzanne Temple. She is waiting in the detective section. The EVIDENCE TECHNICIAN, at your request, has conducted a GSR test on Temple's hands. He used GSR kit #01318 to test for the presence of antimony and barium, two gunpowder elements not commonly present in the environment.

At one time, a AA/GRS kit was used for all ammunition larger than .22 caliber and .22 cartridges made by the Federal Cartridge Company. On the other hand, if the caliber was unknown a SEM/GSR kit was used. Today, no distinction is made; Temple, then, was tested by a combined AA-SEM/GSR kit, now referred to as a GSR kit.

You had not directed the police officer who transported Temple to the police station to place paper bags on her hands (a measure taken to prevent contamination of the hands and subsequent results, though not with Temple because she was not then officially a suspect). Temple, however, told the EVIDENCE TECHNICIAN that she had not washed her hands since about 6:30 the previous evening. Of course, the EVIDENCE TECHNICIAN took samples as soon as possible and avoided touching Temple's hands with his own during the sampling.

Currently, bags are not used because most paper bags are recyclable and contain properties that could contaminate GSR test results. Plastic bags, too, are a problem because hands sweat. Consequently, other avenues are being explored.

Temple sits looking pensive, unconsciously shredding the sides of a white styrofoam coffee cup. She looks up and acknowledges you. It occurs to you that if what the NEIGHBORS said is accurate, the lady looking up at you is likely the murderer. You ask her to accompany you to an interview room that is set up to tape record your conversation.

All police stations have certain rooms which are wired for sound. There usually is an adjoining room which houses the recorder and headphones so that others can listen in on the interview or interrogation. So even though the interview room looks plain, hidden somewhere is a listening device which is recording yours and the suspect's words.

You are an experienced detective. The suspect, you assume, is anxious to get on with the question-answer routine and, so, you are not prone to irrelevant chit-chat. After expressing your genuine sympathy about the death of her husband, you ask some preliminary questions and learn that she and her husband were married for seven years, had no children and worked together typing medical reports.

At this point you are anxious to move on to the matter at hand, anxious to learn what your suspect might say that will help identify the murderer of her husband. You advise Temple of her *Miranda* rights. She says she understands her constitutional rights, waives them and is willing to talk with you.

The day her husband was murdered was much like any other day. She and Alex worked and both took a bowling lesson. Alex went to the mountains to shoot beer cans with a friend whom she had never met. She delivered some typed medical records. On her way home she picked up a burrito for Alex's dinner. Later, about 9:00 p.m., she left the townhouse to go bowling, took the freeway, discovered she had taken the wrong car (the one without her bowling equipment), went back home, saw the neighbors, talked about hearing gun shots, left, bowled until 11:00 p.m., returned home, found husband, went crazy, called 911, looked for cat, rushed to the neighbors. Husband dead.

You suggest she back up and tell you once again how her previous day went. Obligingly, on replay she presents a more precise chronology. Accordingly, you, too, interject a more precise questioning to obtain a more detailed response. (The truth is in the details and lies usually surface from details.)

Marital problems? None.

Arguments? Not that day.

Gun shots? Heard none.

Nervous with neighbors? In a hurry.

Bloody shorts in the bathroom? That time of the month.

Bloody paper towels in the truck? Don't know. Blocked things out. Don't know. Don't know.

Feeling cornered. "I think that you're telling me, I need to see a lawyer. You don't believe what I am telling you. I'd like to have a lawyer."

"It's your choice when you want to talk to a lawyer," you say, but press on because you sense she may break and confess to the murder. Not so. Temple continues to deny any involvement. But you're a patient person, so you methodically prepare the necessary paper work to complete the booking procedure. You take it step-by-step and, in the interim, you continue to discuss the untimely death of her husband. Your patience pays off.

Temple blurts out that she shot her husband because he was "being mean to me." She asks for some tissues.

You nod. "About the gun," you probe.

She continues. "On the way back from the bowling alley, I pulled off the side of the freeway and threw it out the car window."

You hand her a few tissues and ask that she please start from the beginning.

*I was about to leave when someone called. Alex had been working at the computer and took the call in our office. Someone told him that we were behind in our payments and Alex blamed me for screwing up the checking account, for not sending the taxes in on time and for losing clients. When I walked into the bedroom, which is across from where my husband was sitting, he continued to yell at me. When I saw the gun on the dresser, I reminded him that he wasn't so perfect—that he left a loaded gun lying around. I picked up the gun to show him, pointed it in his direction and then it just went off and struck him in the back of the head.*

*Then my husband stood up and roared. He ran around the room and kept yelling my name. I was right in front of him, and he acted as if he couldn't see me. I was so scared, I ran downstairs with the gun in my hands.*

*I was in the living room when I realized my husband had come down behind me. He went to the kitchen, grabbed a towel and put it over the spot where he had been shot. But he kept yelling, "look what you did to me," over and over. I tried to help him; I grabbed some paper towels that were on the microwave and tried to wipe the blood from the side of his head, but he grabbed me and shook me. He kept swearing at me for shooting him in the head.*

*I asked him to let me go, not to hurt me. When the gun went off, he let go of me. While he was running away, the gun kept going off. I didn't know how many times the gun went off, but when Alex stopped making noises I got scared. After that, I turned off the lights in the living room and left.*

*When I left my house, I had the gun in my hand, so I ran to my car. But I forgot that my bowling ball was in the truck. When I went back for the keys, I hid the gun in some bushes. After I ducked the neighbors, I grabbed the gun, put it with the paper towels under the front seat of the truck and drove to the bowling alley. When I got there, I hid the bullets under some bushes in the parking lot.*

Temple agrees to show you and your partner where she hid the bullets and where she threw the gun. She tells you she is telling the truth. She remembers everything about the previous day. "Do you remember asking for a lawyer?" you ask. She says she does but, even so, she still wants to talk to you and still thinks she needs a lawyer.

You clarify her statement. "Since you talked to me after you asked for a lawyer, did you do so voluntarily?" Temple says she did.

At this point you conclude the interrogation. Your partner takes Temple out to the hallway while you remove the cassette tape from the recorder in the adjoining room. You label the cassette, write the case number and suspect's name. You put the cassette tape in your desk and add a reminder to your list of "things to do" to (1) make duplicate tapes and (2) to ask the department secretary to prepare transcripts. Copies of each must be given to the DA and defense attorney. Now, it's time to locate the real evidence.

If the accused's *Miranda* rights are violated <u>but</u> additional statements made concerning the whereabouts of other evidence are voluntarily, the seizure of that evidence is legal. There is no "fruits of the poisonous tree" attached to a *Miranda* violation. *Miranda* protects an individual against self-incrimination, evidence from a verbal statement. Evidence found outside the self-incrimination is legal.

Outside the bowling alley where Temple had bowled, hidden by dense shrubs in a large planter, you find one live .38 caliber bullet. Close by are four expended casings. You photograph, collect and package them.

The area of the freeway where the gun had been thrown, you discover, is very steep. Too steep for two detectives in dress clothes and shoes. However, with the help of the Search and Rescue unit (outfitted in overalls and boots) the black 2" Taurus .38 caliber five shot handgun is quickly found. The gun and the immediate area are photographed; subsequently, the gun, now recovered, is booked into evidence at the police station along with the bullet and casings. Murder suspect, Suzanne Temple, is transported to the police station. She is booked for murder.

Name _____          Date _____

## QUESTIONS - CHAPTER THREE

1. Why did you order a GSR test on Suzanne Temple?

2. Why did you tape record Suzanne Temple's statement?

3. Did you violate *Miranda* by continuing your interrogation after Suzanne asked for an attorney?

Name _____          Date _____

**QUESTIONS - CHAPTER 3 CONTINUED**

4.  After the interrogation, what evidence did Suzanne Temple help you find?

5.  Was the gun and bullet evidence legally seized?

Name _____          Date _____

## QUESTIONS - CHAPTER 3 CONTINUED

6. What steps did you take in collecting the gun and bullet evidence, and why is it important to take these steps?

7. Does the crime scene evidence match the evidence found at the bowling alley and from the freeway embankment? Explain.

# Chapter 4

# The Autopsy: Gunshot Wounds and Cyanide

The body of Alex Temple, unembalmed and refrigerated, is that of an adult male in his late twenties. Identification is confirmed by toe tags. You and your partner are there to observe the autopsy. On the autopsy table, the length of the body from crown of head to heels is determined to be 72 inches. Rigor mortis is present. The head is covered with brown curly hair, left ear lobe pierced. Facial area is clean shaven. Extremities are normal. Tan lines are present on the mid-thighs and at the waist. Overall, Temple's body is lean and muscular.

The DEPUTY MEDICAL EXAMINER begins tape recording that she is entering the body areas through the standard front upper body "Y" shaped incision. She adds that she is making additional incisions down the back in order to explore the path and course of gunshot wound (GSW) #4.

The following projectiles are located in the victim's body by the DEPUTY MEDICAL EXAMINER and, in accordance with chain of custody, are documented in the Forensic Science Center Evidence Report and <u>handed</u> to the CORONER'S EVIDENCE TECHNICIAN:

1. A small irregular fragment of a lead bullet, embedded in the skull (GSW #1), is retrieved and placed in an appropriately labeled and sealed envelope.

2. A medium caliber lead bullet without a jacket, a concave base and slight deformity at the tip, is retrieved from the victim's upper left back (GSW #2). The bullet is placed in an appropriately labeled and sealed envelope.

   (No projectile is retrieved from GSW #3 to the middle left back. This was a through-and-through wound exiting on the left side of Alex's chest.)

3. A medium lead bullet without a jacket and a slight deformed concave base is retrieved from the lower left back (GSW #4). It is placed in an appropriately labeled and sealed envelope.

   (No projectile is retrieved from the GSW #5, a through-and-through wound to the upper left arm. In addition, no soot (tattooing) is seen around any of the entrance wounds which indicates that these injuries were <u>not</u> contact wounds.)

The CORONER'S EVIDENCE TECHNICIAN describes in the report what the three projectile envelopes contain, documents the time and date received, then signs out the bullet evidence.

This evidence will be stored in the Coroner's Evidence Room and then sent by courier to the law enforcement's forensic crime lab to be analyzed by firearm experts. (Sometimes the investigating officer will pickup the evidence and deliver it to the crime lab.)

The stomach, which has been perforated by a bullet is distended by approximately 700 grams of pasty tan material in which there are recognizable fragments of white matter (possibly flour tortilla), meat and beans.

Blood and urine have been extracted and will be submitted to the laboratory. Stomach contents will also be submitted to the laboratory.

Temple, the DEPUTY MEDICAL EXAMINER determines, was shot four times with round nose bullets which caused five wounds. He died from the following gunshot wounds: one to the head, three to the back and one to the left arm. She further determines that the bullet creating the through-and-through wound (GSW #5) could be responsible for the back wound (GSW #4). Four of the wounds were fatal or potentially fatal. They perforated the brain, the stomach, the left lung and the heart. The DEPUTY MEDICAL EXAMINER also determined that the manner of death was at the hands of another (murder).

The chain of custody for the toxicological specimens begins. The DEPUTY MEDICAL EXAMINER records that she is collecting the blood, the pericardial sac of the heart, the bile, the urine and the stomach contents.

These items are documented in the Forensic Science Center Evidence report as having been received and signed out by the EVIDENCE TECHNICIAN.

These items will be taken to the Coroner's Toxicological Lab to be analyzed by toxicological experts.

Subsequent to the autopsy, the DEPUTY MEDICAL EXAMINER will confirm the chain of custody in her typed autopsy report.

Four days after the autopsy, the deceased's sister leaves a message on your voice mail asking you to call her. She sounds anxious.

When you return her call, it's apparent that she has been waiting by the phone for you to return her call. She sounds relieved and you're glad that, as a matter of course, you return calls quickly whenever possible.

Breathlessly, she explains that she was at her brother's apartment, picking up some of his personal effects, when she found a book titled, *Deadly Doses*. "You have to see the book," she tells you. "It's packed with incriminating stuff. I think Suzanne was planning to poison Alex."

*Deadly Doses*, you learn, is not to be taken lightly, particularly the pages earmarked with yellow paper markers. Turning to those pages, you see that they describe poisons that cause death and the doses needed. The book also describes reaction time and approximate time death occurs.

One page especially catches your attention because the top corner has been folded and a word has been underlined. Upon closer inspection, you learn that the page describes a poison that causes death immediately. Cyanide.

> Receiving the book (now evidence) from the sister does not violate any privacy rights (4th Amendment) of Suzanne Temple. A private party is not held to the same search and seizure standards as police; therefore, Alex Temple's sister did not need a search warrant to enter the townhouse and take the book. The evidence seizure was lawful.

You waste no time securing a search warrant to search the townhouse a second time for evidence that will assist you in determining if Temple had continued a plan to murder her husband. This time around, you are searching for the following corroborating evidence:

1. Receipt for a book called *Deadly Doses*.

2. Books, articles or similar items on death or murder.

3. Notes, letters or notations that detail death or murder or chronicle a plan to commit murder or cause of death.

4. Poisons or drugs that appear to have been recently purchased or acquired.

The scope of this second search is narrow. Poisons and drugs are no doubt the gold-star items you hope to find, but equally telling—that Temple had prepared a plan to commit murder—would be her paper trail.

By mid-afternoon, you and two other detectives have seized more than a dozen computer disks, eight murder mysteries, Temple's handwritten notes describing various murder scenarios, as well as a VISA receipt signed by Temple for *Deadly Doses*. Your search, unfortunately, uncovers no poison.

> Search warrant safety measures, like those required for arresting an outstanding suspect, were not under consideration. The townhouse was empty and the other detectives were with you only to help search for items of evidence.

The next day, after a five-day lapse, you return to the coroner's office to fill out a supplemental toxicology request to test the victim's blood for poison. The TOXICOLOGIST administered an analysis for heavy metals and cyanide.

The results were conclusive; the victim had a toxic level of cyanide in his blood.

COUNTY OF LOS ANGELES

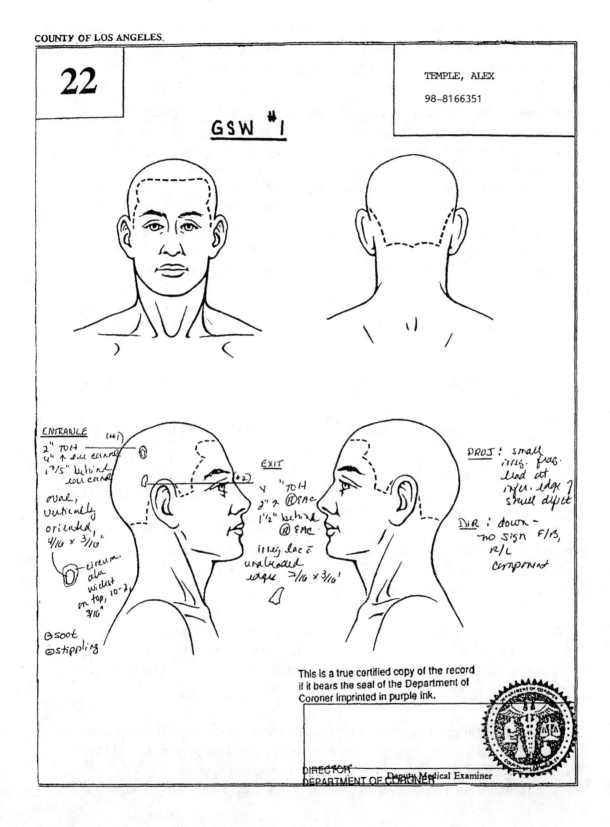

**22**

TEMPLE, ALEX

98–8166351

GSW #1

ENTRANCE          (H1)
2" TOH
4" ↑ ext canal
i 7/5" behind
    ear canal

oval,
vertically
oriented,
4/16 × 3/16"

○ — circum.
    abr.
    widest
    on top, 10–2
    3/16"

⊖ soot
⊖ stippling

EXIT          (+7)
Y "TOH
2" ↑ @ EAC
1½" behind
@ EAC

irreg lac c̄
unabraded
edge 7/16 × 3/16"

PROJ: small
irreg. frag.
lead at
infer. edge ?
skull defect

DIR: down-
no sign F/B,
R/L
component

This is a true certified copy of the record
if it bears the seal of the Department of
Coroner imprinted in purple ink.

DIRECTOR
DEPARTMENT OF CORONER          Deputy Medical Examiner

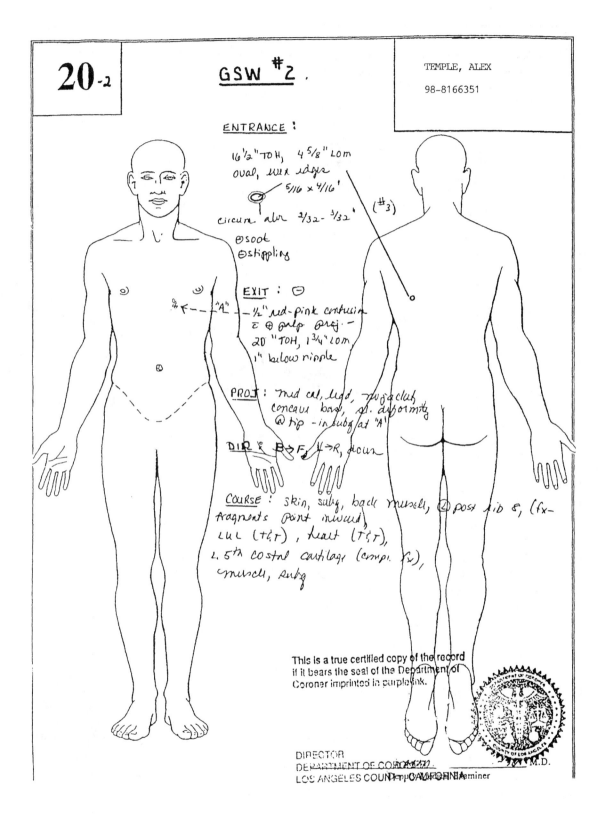

**20**-2

GSW #2.

TEMPLE, ALEX
98-8166351

ENTRANCE:

16½" TO H, 4⅝" LOM
oval, well edges
5/16 × 4/16'
circum abr 2/32 - 3/32'
⊖ soot
⊖ stippling

(#3)

EXIT: ⊖

"A" — ½" red-pink contusion
c̄ ⊕ pulp proj -
20 "TOH, 1¾" LOM
1" below nipple

PROJ: med cal, ligd, no jacket,
concave base, sl. deformity
@ tip - in subg at "A"

DIR: B→F, L→R, down

COURSE: skin, subg, back muscle, ② post rib 8, (fx-
fragments point inward),
LUL (t & r), heart (t & r),
L 5th costal cartilage (compl. fx),
muscle, subg

DIRECTOR
DEPARTMENT OF CORONER
LOS ANGELES COUNTY, CALIFORNIA   M.D.
Chief Medical Examiner

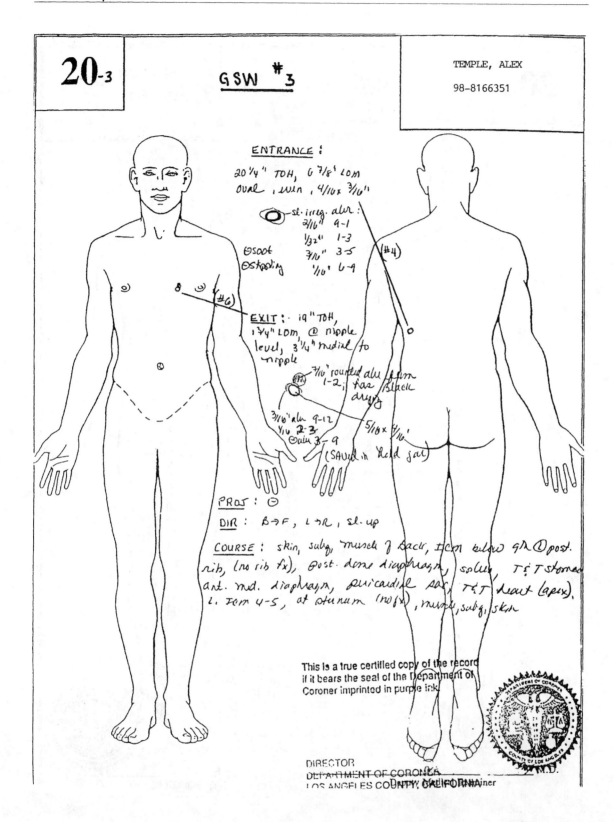

**20-3**

GSW #3

TEMPLE, ALEX

98-8166351

ENTRANCE :

20¼" TOH, 6 ⅞" LOM
oval, wen, 4/16 x 3/16"

— st. irreg. abr :
        3/16"   9-1
        1/32"   1-3
⊖soot   3/16"   3-5
⊖stippling   1/16"   6-9

(#6)

(#4)

EXIT : 19" TOH,
1¾" LOM @ nipple
level, 3¼" medial to
nipple

7/16" rounded abr from
1-2; has black
drying

3/16" abr 9-12
4/16" 2-3
⊖abr 3-9          5/16 x 4/16"

(Saved in held jar)

PROJ : ⊖

DIR : B→F, L→R, sl. up

COURSE : skin, subq, muscle of back, 1cm below 9R ⊕ post.
rib, (no rib fx), post. dome diaphragm, spleen, T&T stomach,
ant. med. diaphragm, pericardial sac, T&T heart (apex),
L. 1cm 4-5, at sternum (no fx), muscle, subq, skin

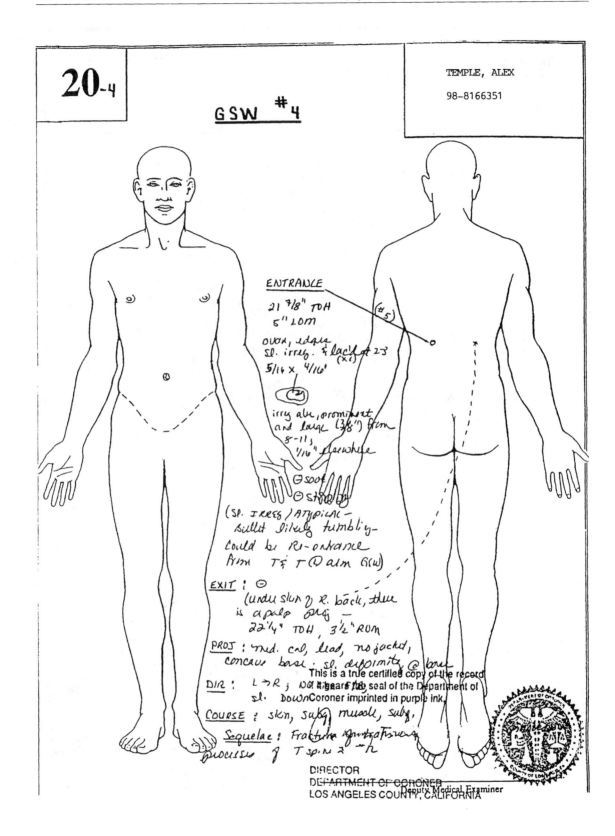

**20**-4

GSW #4

TEMPLE, ALEX

98-8166351

ENTRANCE

21 7/8" TOH

5" LOM

ovar, edge

sl. irreg. & lack at 23 (x1)

5/16 x 4/16"

(2)

irreg abr, prominent and large (3/8") from 8-11; 1/16" elsewhere

⊖ soot

⊖ stipple

(SL. IRREG / ATYPICAL — bullet likely tumbling — could be RE-entrance from T & T @ alm G(w))

EXIT: ⊖ (under skin of R. back, there is a palp proj — 22 1/4" TOH, 3 1/2" RUM

PROJ: med. cal, lead, no jacket, concave base; sl. deformity @ base

DIR: L → R; slightly down

COURSE: skin, subq, muscle, subq,

Sequelae: Fracture / contusions / processes of T sp. N 2 - R

**20**

## GSW #5

TEMPLE, ALEX

98-8166351

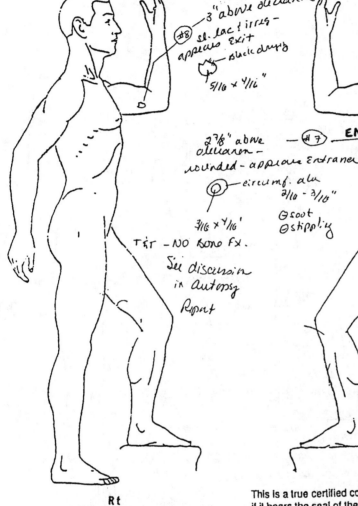

EXIT

#8 — 3" above olecranon
sl. lac + irreg -
appears Exit
— black drng
5/16 x 4/16"

2 7/8" above
olecranon —
rounded — appears Entrance     #7 — ENTRANCE
— circumf. abr
2/16 - 3/16"
⊕ soot
⊕ stippling

3/16 x 4/16"

T&T — NO bono FX.

See discussion
in Autopsy
Report

Rt

DIRECTOR
DEPARTMENT OF CORONER
LOS ANGELES COUNTY, CALIFORNIA

Name _____          Date _____

## QUESTIONS - CHAPTER FOUR

1. What evidence did the Deputy Medical Examiner find as a result of Alex Temple's autopsy?

2. Can you establish the sequence of shots sustained by Alex Temple?

3. Explain the chain of custody for the evidence from the autopsy.

Name _____        Date _____

## QUESTIONS - CHAPTER 4 CONTINUED

4.  What did Alex Temple's sister discover and what impact does this evidence have on your investigation?

5.  Did Temple's sister legally seize the book, *Deadly Doses*, from the Temple's townhouse? Explain.

6.  Why did you secure another search warrant for the Temple's townhouse?

*Chapter 5*

# The First Trial

The Deputy District Attorney (DA), a thoughtful, slender man of medium height, in anticipation of Suzanne Temple's upcoming trial, is confident that a first degree murder conviction will be handed down. Indeed, his judicial stats, impressive by anyone's professional standards, speak for themselves. Moreover, he is certain that Suzanne Temple is guilty. He has lay witnesses to testify that they heard a woman scream, heard shots and, subsequently, saw Suzanne leave the apartment. He has competent police officers and skilled evidence technicians who found real evidence, including the murder weapon. He also has expert witnesses who analyzed the evidence and their conclusions pointed to Suzanne Temple. Moreover, the presiding JUDGE of the courtroom where the Deputy District Attorney has been assigned is a substantially tenured jurist and capable of moving trials smoothly along. Then there is you. The DA has the relentless homicide detective to whom Suzanne Temple confessed the murder.

The DA and JUDGE has designated you INVESTIGATING OFFICER (IO) and, so, you will sit next to the DA during the entire trial. Legal procedures mandate that witnesses wait outside the courtroom, but as the IO, you will be allowed to sit in trial and listen to witness testimony even though you, too, will be asked to testify.

On the first day of trial, before the courtroom opens, you meet the evidence custodian at the police department and request the evidence items. Before you sign for their release, you quickly review the list. No cassette tape of Suzanne Temple's interrogation? Can't be! You recall making copies of the original and distributing them. But the original? You must have misread the list. You run your finger down the list, repeat each item aloud in your head. No tape. Nonetheless, you sign the release slip and put the evidence items in a large paper bag. However, before you walk to the courthouse, you race to your office and check your desk drawers. No tape. You check with the department secretary who typed the transcripts. She remembers that you gave her a duplicate and that she gave it back to you. No tape. You race to your detective unit and check the glove compartment and the trunk. No tape.

At the courthouse, you use a pay-phone and call home. Tape with Temple written on it? No tape.

You find the DA in his office. He is deep in thought, unconsciously toying with his thin black mustache. He senses your presence and looks up. Though he appears sharp-eyed this morning, his dark brown eyes are noticeably blood-shot. Reluctantly, you tell him that you've misplaced the original tape. He contemplates a second, shrugs, then in a matter-of-fact way says he'll tell the DEFENSE attorney. This private counsel hired by the defendant, he says, appears to be a single-minded, stern defender. Her impeccable, hair-in-place demeanor lacks any semblance of flexibility. Still, he hopes, that since she has a copy she won't ask for a separate hearing on the issue of the lost original tape. Unquestionably, this aggressive DEFENSE attorney will slap your hand in front of the JURORS, will embarrass you, but once that is behind you, the DA tells you, she will provide you with her copy for the JURORS to hear.

The DA moves on to the other evidence and asks to see it. You take out the baseball cap, the wallet, the credit cards and bullet projectile that were taken from the murder scene. You also have the gun that was taken from the freeway embankment and the ammunition that was in the master bedroom, as well as receipts for both. The bullet and casings that were found at the bowling alley, the bullet projectiles and the bullet fragments that were removed from Alex Temple's body during the autopsy are in the paper bag. Moreover, you have *Deadly Doses* and the bookstore receipt. The videotape of the crime scene is there too. And, last, the blood evidence. The DA had asked you to take the blood evidence to court even though he and the DEFENSE are expected to stipulate (to agree) that the blood belongs to Alex Temple; he did this because sometimes attorneys—strategically—reevaluate a stipulation, then reconsider their previous agreement to stipulate.

During the trial, you will be called upon to escort the DA's witnesses into the courtroom who will testify about what they heard or saw the evening that Alex Temple was murdered, as well as how the Temples acted prior to the murder and how Suzanne Temple acted subsequent to the murder. The witnesses include the 911 OPERATOR, the NEIGHBOR, the MANAGER, the BOWLING PROFESSIONAL, and Suzanne's BOWLING PARTNER. The NEIGHBOR'S GIRLFRIEND and DAUGHTER have moved out-of-state, and the DA decided not to fly them back for this open/shut case.

Today, in court, the DA begins "laying foundation" by calling the police department's EVIDENCE TECHNICIAN, his first witness.

In order for evidence or expert testimony to be accepted by the court, a foundation must be laid. The attorney must prove that the real evidence presented in court is the same evidence taken during the investigation. To do this, the original collector, as well as those who analyzed the evidence, are called to testify. This is the evidence chain-of-custody. Expert testimony is different. The attorney must convince the JUDGE that the expert is, indeed, an expert. To do this the attorney relies on the expert's training and experience. The opposing attorney will try to challenge the witness's expertise through the voir dire process. The opposing attorney will ask questions of the witness and attack him/her to try and convince the JUDGE that the witness is not, in fact, an expert.

The TECHNICIAN is waiting in the witness room, just outside the courtroom. You peek in. "You're up," you say.

He stops reading his report, shuffles it back into chronological order and stretches some before rising. He walks into the courtroom. You follow. You sense the JURORS' eyes are on you and the TECHNICIAN. You find your seat. The TECHNICIAN stops just before the witness stand. He has made this walk many times and knows to face the court CLERK. Both raise their right hands.

"Do you solemnly swear to tell the truth, the whole truth and nothing but the truth so help you God?" She asks.

"I do," says the TECHNICIAN.

"Please take the stand and spell your full name."

Before any questions are asked, the DA advises the JUDGE, a distinguished white-haired jurist, that he and the DEFENSE have reached a stipulation regarding the blood. They both agree as to the disposition of the blood recovered at the crime scene by this witness and that the blood withdrawn from Alex Temple's body during the autopsy was the blood used to make the comparisons. This, then, eliminates the need for further proof that the blood on the baseball cap, blood droplets on the chair and magazine, blood on the fingerprint, blood on the paper towels found in the car and the blood on the seat adjuster was the same blood type as Alex Temple's. (The DEFENSE stipulated to this evidence because Suzanne Temple is prepared to take the witness stand in her own defense and admit to killing her husband; this, then, eliminates the need to challenge the blood evidence.)

The JUDGE accepts the stipulation and, after clearing his throat some, carefully explains the stipulation to the JURY:

A stipulation is an agreement between the prosecuting and defense attorneys that certain fact(s) occurred, that it is relevant evidence and, because they stipulate, there is no need to prove the fact(s). Therefore, there is no need to call the witness or witnesses to testify about these facts.

In place of their testimony, the attorney reads into the record what the witness or witnesses *would* testify to if called to the witness stand.

He tells the DA to proceed.

"May I approach the witness your honor?"

Given permission to approach the witness, The DA elicits the TECHNICIAN's qualifications: education, work experience and training. He is a college graduate and a veteran. He has been employed by the police department as an evidence technician for seven years and has processed hundreds of crime scenes and many homicide scenes. In addition, he received crime scene training through various accredited programs.

The DA turns to you and asks for the videotape. You open the bag and remove a 9" X 12" evidence envelope: "Crime Scene Video" is written on the front.

The DA allows the DEFENSE to scrutinize the exhibit.

He approaches the witness and hands him the same package.

"Do you recognize this package?" The DA asks.

"Yes, I do, answers the TECHNICIAN.

What is the package?"

"It's a police department's evidence envelope; it contains a VHS tape of the crime scene."

"How do you know this?" The DA asks.

"I videotaped the crime scene, then placed the video in the evidence envelope and marked it with my initials."

"Can you please explain to the court the procedure that followed the taping of the crime scene."

"I removed the videotape from the camera, labeled the tape and wrote the case number, the address of the scene and my name on it. I also packaged the tape in this envelope and sealed it. I wrote the case number, the crime scene address and the description of the evidence (videotape) on the front and then booked it into evidence."

"Please explain to the JURY what you mean by 'booked it into evidence'?"

"I took the evidence to the evidence custodian at the police station. She received the evidence and logged it into the evidence room."

"Do you recognize the handwriting?"

"Yes, I do. It's mine," the TECHNICIAN answers.

The TECHNICIAN is asked to open the envelope and remove the videotape as well as describe for the court reporter what he is doing.

"Can you be sure the tape is that of the crime scene?"

"Yes, the label on the videotape has the information I wrote."

The DA, through questioning, gets a brief overview of what the tape depicts. The DA requests the court's permission to show the tape to the JURY. Since the DEFENSE has already seen the tape, they have no objections.

The tape presents the entire townhouse, specifically the partially opened sliding glass door, the window screen leaning against the wall, Alex Temple's body, the wallet, the scattered credit cards, the blood and blood items, disheveled drawers in the upstairs bedroom. Also on the tape are the exterior patio and parking area.

"In your opinion, did this appear to be a burglary?"

"Yes, it did," the TECHNICIAN answered. "The place was messy and somewhat disturbed."

The DA marks the tape People's "Exhibit 1" and requests that the JUDGE enter it into evidence.

Also introduced is the victim's leather wallet, credit cards and baseball cap. The EVIDENCE TECHNICIAN testifies that although leather can be dusted for fingerprints, only the credit cards inside were processed for latent fingerprints and no prints were found. Following the custody procedure, he explains to the JURY, that he removed the credit cards from the evidence room, took the cards to his lab and he then processed them for latent prints. Thereafter, he placed the credit cards back inside the evidence envelope, resealed it and then booked the cards back into evidence. These items are marked People's "Exhibit 2 and Exhibit 3."

The DA asks the TECHNICIAN to open the evidence envelope and remove the baseball cap. The TECHNICIAN testifies where he saw the baseball cap and how he packaged the item. He shows the JURY the cap and points out the bullet hole. This item is marked People's "Exhibit 4."

> Blood evidence is handled differently in court. Bloody items can be brought to court but cannot generally be opened because of the alleged health risks associated with blood. In this case, the exception applied because the DA effectively argued that the JURY needed to see the bullet hole in the cap. The JUDGE allowed for this but mandated that the EVIDENCE TECHNICIAN wear gloves and use a pencil to point out the bullet hole. After the baseball cap was returned to the envelope and the envelope resealed, the gloves and pencil were destroyed. Though the JUDGE accepted the cap into evidence, he will not allow the JURY to re-examine it during deliberation.

Lastly, the EVIDENCE TECHNICIAN testifies that on the night of the homicide you directed him to conduct a Gunshot Residue (GSR) test on Suzanne Temple. He says that the GSR swabbing took place at the police station. The TECHNICIAN explains how he used the GSR evidence kit to swab Suzanne's hands to test for the presence of antimony and barium, gunpowder elements not commonly present in the environment. The kit was labeled #01318, as were the two small plastic tubes containing two swabs each. The TECHNICIAN explained that he examined the labels carefully to make sure all the numbers corresponded. Before removing one of the swabs from the tube labeled RIGHT BACK, he slipped on plastic gloves. Careful not to touch the swab to any surface, he held the swab in his left hand and with his right hand lightly sprayed the back of Temple's right hand with 5% nitric acid, using the sprayer provided.

The DA interjects. "Will you explain to the JURY why you use nitric acid?"

"It detects gunpowder."

The TECHNICIAN went on to say that he swabbed Temple's right hand, swabbing in one direction from the ends of her fingers to the wrist, concentrating on the thumb, the forefinger and the web area between—the areas where gunpowder elements will normally settle when a person fires a handgun.

After that, he said, he removed the second swab from the same tube, replaced it with the first swab, sprayed the front of the defendant's hand just enough to moisten it, swabbed it again, then placed the second swab in the tube and sealed it tightly.

The TECHNICIAN looked down at his report a few seconds, then resumed. "The procedure was repeated on the left hand. After that, I put the tubes into a GRS evidence envelope and then placed the GSR kit into evidence to be analyzed by a criminalist.

On cross-examination, the DEFENSE receives permission to approach the witness.

"About my client's alleged burglary set up," she begins. "Isn't it true that burglars usually force their way into a home?" She asks the EVIDENCE TECHNICIAN.

"Usually? Yes," he responds.

"Was there forced entry at this home?"

"No."

"Have you responded to other homes where the occupants were messy?"

"Yes."

"Where drawers were opened and the items inside were scattered?"

"Yes."

"To the best of your knowledge was anything taken from the Temple's townhouse?"

"No."

The DEFENSE attorney pauses, walks toward the 12 jurors and surveys them left to right for their full attention. "Then, is it possible that the Temples are merely messy and that no burglary setup occurred?"

"It's possible."

Standing behind you now she asks, "Isn't it true that a *burglary setup* was really only this DETECTIVE'S opinion?"

"No. It was my thought as well."

The EVIDENCE TECHNICIAN also testifies that he fingerprinted the living room window, where the screen had been detached and the patio sliding glass door, but found no fingerprints, smudges or glove prints.

The EVIDENCE TECHNICIAN reseals the evidence envelope and writes his name, then dates the envelope next to the tape. The DA hands the evidence to the CLERK for storage.

When evidence is received by the court, the CLERK is like the evidence custodian at the police department, so to speak, the court's evidence custodian.

The DA calls for more stipulations. The SENIOR CRIMINALIST from the CRIME LAB *would* testify that she received Suzanne Temple's GSR kit, analyzed the eight swabs and found levels of antimony and barium which are consistent with handling or firing a firearm.

The FINGERPRINT EXPERT from the police department *would* take the stand and testify that she received the water heater cabinet door with the bloody fingerprint from the EVIDENCE TECHNICIAN and after comparing the print to Suzanne Temple's booking prints, eliminated her as the person who left that print. It is further stipulated that the bloody fingerprint was left by Alex Temple.

The next stipulation concerns the blue, female jean shorts taken from the bathroom of the townhouse. The DA states that, "the shorts belonging to Suzanne Temple, appeared blood stained and were submitted to the CRIME LAB for analysis to determine if the blood was menstrual blood or if the blood belonged to Alex Temple, but the blood was never analyzed."

It is also stipulated that Suzanne Temple's FRIEND *would* testify that, the living room window screen was off because, earlier in the week, the Temples had locked themselves out of their townhouse, and Alex Temple climbed into the living room through that window.

The DEPUTY MEDICAL EXAMINER is called by the DA. She testifies that Alex Temple's death was caused by multiple gunshot wounds and that the massive dark purple lividity was consistent with that type of death. She says that she removed two medium caliber bullet projectiles from GSWs #2 and #4 (body shots) and a bullet fragment from GSW #1 (head shot). She explains that GSW #3 was a through-and-through wound, so no projectile was recovered. (This was recovered at the scene.) GSW #5, she says, was a through-and-through wound to Temple's left arm. The DEPUTY MEDICAL EXAMINER believes that GSW #4 was the same bullet which passed through GSW #5. (A diagram is used to show the trajectories of the bullets which reinforces her theory of GSWs #4 and #5.) She further explains that the bullets were given to the CORONER EVIDENCE TECHNICIAN for packaging and transportation to the crime lab.

The DEPUTY MEDICAL EXAMINER also confirms that Temple's blood was sent to toxicology for cyanide presence and that the test showed positive for that poison.

On cross-examination, the DEFENSE attempts to discount the death by cyanide allegation; she confirms that the MEDICAL EXAMINER neither observed pink lividity nor pink tone to the lips and nails of the body. The MEDICAL EXAMINER testifies that cyanide poisoning is rarely a method for murder but, nonetheless, she would expect to recognize the pinkish warnings in that type of death. In addition, the MEDICAL EXAMINER testifies that an almond-like odor may accompany death by cyanide upon opening the body cavities. None was present.

Only 50 percent of the population can smell this almond-like odor and, of this percentage, most are women.

The DEFENSE produces autopsy photographs of the body's lips, nails and lividity, which were brought in by the MEDICAL EXAMINER. "These areas of the body are purple which are inconsistent with cyanide poisoning." The MEDICAL EXAMINER is shown her autopsy report; she authenticates it, and the report is marked as People's "Exhibit 5."

More stipulations. The JUDGE's cheek is resting comfortably against his left fingers. When the DA addresses him, he turns. The DA advises him that he and the

DEFENSE have stipulated that the CORONER EVIDENCE TECHNICIAN *would* testify that he took the bullets from the DEPUTY MEDICAL EXAMINER, packaged each separately and sent them via courier to the Los Angeles County Crime Lab to the Firearms section. In addition, the CORONER INVESTIGATOR *would* testify that he took GSR swabs of Alex Temple's hands at the murder scene. Those swabs were packaged and sent to the Coroner's lab for analysis. To complete the chain-of-custody, the CORONER GSR EXPERT *would* also testify that the GSR evidence package was received, that the swabs were analyzed and that levels of antimony and barium, associated with gunshot residue, were found on Alex Temple's palms. The GSR EXPERT documents and submits a report that is marked People's "Exhibit 6."

The DA calls the TOXICOLOGIST INTERN from the Coroner's office. He testifies that during the autopsy, he withdrew blood from Alex Temple's body, placed the blood in a tube laced with the preservative sodium fluoride, sealed the tube, wrote case information on the attached label and submitted it to a TOXICOLOGIST.

The TOXICOLOGIST, a recognized expert in the toxicology field, takes the stand. He testifies that when he conducted a drug scan and cyanide test on Alex Temple's blood, he found no presence of drugs but found a 1.20 UG/ML (micrograms per milliliter) level of cyanide—potentially lethal.

On cross-examination, the DEFENSE verifies that no additional tests were conducted in Los Angeles to make certain of the cyanide finding. The DEFENSE further establishes that the blood was kept refrigerated at the coroners (an important issue in cyanide preservation) and that part of that blood was released to a San Diego lab at the request of the DEFENSE, then sent to a cyanide expert in northern California.

> Elements that could be found in blood, like cyanide, will evaporate at a far quicker rate if the blood is not preserved with the chemical EDTA <u>and</u> if it is not kept refrigerated. This is why it is important to make sure the container has the chemical agent (a powdery white substance) and that the blood is kept cold.

"Are you familiar with the CYANIDE EXPERT?" The DEFENSE asks the TOXICOLOGIST.

"Yes. He's the foremost expert in cyanide poisoning."

"If the blood that you released to the San Diego lab was received by the CYANIDE EXPERT in northern California two months later, would you expect to find cyanide levels in the blood?"

"Typically, cyanide in the blood will dissipate after an extended period of time. However, if the blood remained preserved and was refrigerated for the two months' duration, I would expect to find some measurable amount of cyanide in the blood."

The DA marks the TOXICOLOGIST EXPERT'S report as an evidence exhibit and hands it to the CLERK.

You are up next. You take the oath, spell your name and disclose your law enforcement bio. The DA asks about your crime scene investigation.

He also asks that you explain to the JURY your reason for requesting a GSR on Suzanne Temple.

About the interrogation. The DA hands you a cassette tape of your taped conversation with Suzanne Temple.

The DA requests that the JURORS be allowed to hear the tape. The JUDGE grants the request, then adjourns for the day. The JUDGE excuses you and orders you back tomorrow at 9:00 a.m. You leave the witness stand and rejoin the DA. The JUDGE excuses the JURY. You, the DA and the DEFENSE ATTORNEY stand as the JURY walks out of the courtroom. Thereafter, the JUDGE leaves through the back door to his chamber.

Rather than return the remaining evidence items to the evidence room, you leave them with the court CLERK.

The next day, you are first to take the stand and are reminded that you are still under oath. The DA asks a couple questions about how and where the interrogation was recorded. The DA touches upon the subject of the lost original and then hands you the duplicate tape.

"Is this the original tape of Suzanne Temple's interview?"

"No."

"What happened to the original tape."

"I somehow misplaced it."

"Did you duplicate the original tape soon after the interview was completed?"

"Yes."

"Is the duplicate tape an accurate copy of the original?"

"Yes."

(The DA brought up the lost tape during direct examination to "take the sting out" of the inevitable cross-examination of this subject and to show the JURY that they have nothing to hide.)

The DA hands you the taped confession. The CLERK provides a tape recorder. You set up the tape and adjust the sound for the JURORS to hear.

When the tape concludes, it is returned to the evidence envelope.

When questioned about the recovery of the bullet and casings, you explain that Suzanne Temple, whom you identify in court, directed you to the bushes under which she hid the evidence. You say that the single bullet and the four expended casing were together under that area outside the bowling alley. The DA hands you an envelope containing the bullet and casings; you remove the items and identify them.

Next, the DA questions you about the recovery of the gun. You explain to the JURY that Suzanne Temple directed you to the freeway overpass and to the brush area where she threw the gun. You add that the .38 caliber Taurus five shot revolver was found within a 200-foot radius of that area. The DA produces a blown up photograph of the overpass. You authenticate the photograph and make an "X" where you found the gun.

The DA hands you an envelope containing the gun. You identify the evidence envelope and remove the gun to show it to the JURY. (You had opened the envelope prior to the start of this court date to show the gun to the bailiff. She inspected the gun to make sure it wasn't loaded.) You further identify the gun by its serial number.

The DA hands you another evidence envelope. This envelope contains the bullet and bullets casings found at the bowling alley. Using the same procedure, you identify these items.

"What did you do with the bullet and casings from the bowling alley and the Taurus gun from the brush by the freeway?" The DA asks.

"I took them to the CRIME LAB, handed them to the FIREARM'S EXPERT, filled out a crime lab receipt and requested that he compare the gun to the bullet evidence."

You are also questioned about finding the *Deadly Doses* book. The DA produces the book. You identify it by turning to the last page and noting your initials on the upper right corner of the page. You tell the JURY that part of the book addresses death by cyanide poisoning; another part deals with death by multiple sources.

The DA hands you a Master Charge receipt from a BOOKSTORE. You identify the receipt that lists *Deadly Doses* as having been purchased and signed for by the defendant. The receipt, you testify, was found inside a drawer.

The DA then hands you a Master Card receipt from a GUN SHOP. You identify the receipt. The receipt, signed by the defendant, details the purchase of a Taurus gun and .38 caliber ammunition.

On cross-examination, the DEFENSE immediately asks you about the lost original tape.

"Wouldn't you agree detective that the preservation of evidence is essential in a criminal investigation?"

"Yes, I agree."

"And the proper chain-of-custody is the best way to preserve evidence?"

"Yes."

"Now, I understand that you lost the original tape of your interrogation of my client. Isn't that true?"

"Yes."

"You never placed the tape into evidence?"

"No."

"Detective, is it your practice to record interrogations?"

"Yes."

"And, isn't it true that information from an interrogation is very important evidence to the DA and the DEFENSE?"

"Yes."

"Since recording interrogations is common practice for you, what do you normally do with the tape?"

"I duplicate the tape and then place the original into evidence."

"But, you didn't use that procedure in this case, did you?"

"In part. I duplicated the tape but never put it into evidence."

"Detective, how many times have you lost a taped interrogation?"

"This was my first time."

"How many times have you failed to place the original tape into evidence?"

"Just this time."

(The DEFENSE succeeds in embarrassing you and rightly so; you screwed up.)

The DEFENSE continues. She begins to attack you regarding the taped confession. She asks that you replay the part where Suzanne Temple asked for an attorney.

"It appears my client asked for an attorney. Is that not so?"

"Yes."

"Did you provide her with one?"

"No."

"So, DETECTIVE, you totally ignored my client's request for counsel and continued to interrogate her."

"No. I told her that it was her choice when she wanted a lawyer. And, later in our talk, I asked her if she had wanted a lawyer before or had it been her choice to continue talking. She said she had wanted to continue talking."

The DEFENSE continues to drill you. You feel that her purpose with this line of questioning is to get the JURORS to dislike you.

"DETECTIVE, the DA and I have stipulated that my client's shorts, the ones found in the bathroom with a stain on them, were sent to the CRIME LAB in order to determine if the stain was a blood stain and, if so, was it Alex Temple's blood. Do you remember this stipulation?"

"Yes."

"Were you the person who sent the shorts to be analyzed."

"Yes."

"And were the shorts analyzed?"

"No, they were not."

"I see. And, as such, we further stipulated that the shorts were never analyzed. Isn't that true?"

"Yes."

"Why, may I ask, were the shorts not analyzed?"

"I don't know."

"Isn't it your responsibility to make sure that everything you want analyzed is analyzed?"

"Yes."

"Did you just forget to follow-up or did you simply ignore this piece of evidence?"

"Neither counselor."

"Then please explain why the shorts were not analyzed."

"I sent the shorts to the CRIME LAB for blood analysis, but later learned that this piece of evidence was overlooked. However, when I was told of the oversight, I chose not to pursue it because I was told that the blood evidence was not at issue." The DEFENSE attorney looks knowingly at the jurors, "An oversight. I see."

Your testimony has ended. The JUDGE asks you to reseal all the evidence items in front of you. They are formally marked as People's Exhibits and handed to the COURT CLERK.

The DA requests that the JUDGE accept the next and last stipulation. He says, "The FIREARM'S EXAMINER of the CRIME LAB would testify that he received a .38 caliber bullet, three .38 caliber bullet casings and a .38 caliber Taurus five shot revolver (stating the serial number) from the DETECTIVE, conducted an analysis using that evidence, as well as the bullets from the autopsy, and determined that the gun was the weapon used to shoot Alex Temple. In addition, this witness would testify that the gun was in good working order with a normal trigger pull."

The DEFENSE wants to stipulate as to her client's purchase of the gun and the ammunition from the GUN STORE, two weeks before the murder. Quite simply, according to the over-the-counter firearms transaction record, the purchase was made. End of conversation.

The DA doesn't buy into that simplistic assertion. Instead, he calls the owner to the stand who testifies that, not only did he sell the gun and accessories to Suzanne Temple, but he also easily remembered Suzanne from a photograph you showed him because very few women buy guns. And, he adds, most women don't know what type of gun they want. Not Mrs. Temple.

"Mrs. Temple was different," he remarks, "She knew *exactly* what she wanted."

The DA wants to show the JURY that for at least two weeks prior to Alex Temple's death, Suzanne Temple planned to kill her husband, planned it down to the very last detail.

The last witness for the DA is a representative of a LIFE INSURANCE COMPANY. The representative tells the JURY that four years ago Alex and Suzanne Temple purchased a $100,000 life insurance policy, and each named the other beneficiary. The DA wants to convince the JURY that by Suzanne's own volition—her testimony to you, the homicide detective—the Temples were in financial trouble. No doubt, Suzanne, who was in charge of the finances, chose to murder her husband for financial gain. (The DEFENSE, on the other hand, wants to convince the JURY that if financial gain had been the motive, her client would have <u>recently</u> increased the policy limits.)

The DA rests.

(The damp tissue found in the truck was tested but nothing was found. Since this item had no relevancy to the case, it was not offered as evidence.)

The DEFENSE has few witnesses.

"The DEFENSE calls the CYANIDE EXPERT."

The CYANIDE EXPERT has an impressive vitae. He testifies that his lab receives work from all over the world. In criminal matters, both prosecutors and defense attorneys request his expertise. In addition, the CYANIDE EXPERT trains toxicologists, evaluates their work and inspects lab facilities.

The DEFENSE establishes that the expert received Alex Temple's blood sample from the SAN DIEGO LAB via Federal Express. The CYANIDE EXPERT tells the JURY that the blood was analyzed for the presence of cyanide using the most updated technological equipment.

"No cyanide detected in the blood," the EXPERT says.

"But," the DEFENSE says, "a cyanide concentration of 1.20 ug/ml was allegedly detected by the coroner's toxicologist. Can you explain that?"

The EXPERT explains that if the blood was properly preserved and refrigerated and even though he received it a year later, he would expect to have detected a presence of cyanide at some level had cyanide poisoning occurred.

On cross-examination, the CYANIDE EXPERT reports that he is being paid by the DEFENSE to testify. The CYANIDE EXPERT also reports that the Coroner's TOXICOLOGIST'S methods were proper.

The DEFENSE calls you as a defense witness. She verifies that no cyanide was found in the townhouse on both occasions that search warrants were served.

"The DEFENSE then calls Suzanne Temple to the stand."

Suzanne Temple admits to killing her husband. She doesn't deviate from the interrogation tape. "He kept humiliating me, blaming me for all our problems."

Suzanne testifies that she was constantly ill because of her responsibility to run the business, make a profit, tend to the housework and, on top of all that, "Alex kept putting pressure on me to become a professional bowler so we could get out of our financial troubles."

Suzanne talks about the shooting. "It was an accident. The gun went off and hit him in the head."

She answers questions about the other shots. "He came after me, so I ran downstairs and tried to get out of his way, but he grabbed me. He pushed me into the dining room and kept shaking me. I was terrified, really terrified. All I know is that the gun kept going off."

_ The DEFENSE questions her about *Deadly Doses*.

"I wanted to commit suicide, but not make it look like suicide."

Suzanne explains that her parents are Catholic and that suicide is not acceptable.

"If they knew that I had committed suicide, they would believe I hadn't gone to Heaven."

The DA attacks Suzanne on cross-examination. He accuses her of planning her husband's murder, poisoning him and, finally, shooting him. He sets up a timetable of what she ate the day of the murder: for breakfast, a bagel; for lunch, a small pasta salad; for dinner, not hungry. Alex? Dinner? "I picked up a burrito for Alex after my errand. Yes, he ate it all. Alex loved burritos. No, I did not plan to murder my husband."

The DA then questions her about setting up a burglary scene at the townhouse. Suzanne admits to removing Alex's wallet, scattering the credit cards and placing the upstairs telephone next to the body. She even admits to opening the drawers to make it look as though someone had gone through them.

"I was scared," Suzanne admits. "I knew I was in trouble."

The DEFENSE PSYCHOLOGIST is called next.

The PSYCHOLOGIST testifies that she interviewed Suzanne Temple more than a dozen times after the homicide. She adds that her opinion of Suzanne's state of mind at the time of the homicide is based on these interviews and tests administered to her. It is also based on reading the police and autopsy reports, interviewing her family for background information and looking at photographs of Suzanne before the homicide.

The PSYCHOLOGIST adds that Suzanne had been chronically depressed for at least two years before the incident took place. "Suzanne's depression was from the following high stressors: financial pressures, a heavy workload, illness, sexual deprivation and verbal abuse from her spouse."

She tells the JURY that Suzanne's test results were very similar to those of battered women and, specifically, to women who kill their batterer during domestic violence. The PSYCHOLOGIST ruled out the possibility that the defendant was capable of "faking."

Another test revealed a "helpless feeling" that is consistent with people contemplating suicide.

The PSYCHOLOGIST testifies that she read *Deadly Doses* and, feels that, coupled with Suzanne's purchase of a gun days before, suicide was quite possibly on her mind.

The PSYCHOLOGIST further testifies that the husband's grabbing and shaking could have resulted in a high intensity of emotion for Suzanne—much more than a normal person—and because of this, she could have experienced "dissociate behavior." Therefore, it is likely she forgot that she pulled the trigger.

The PSYCHOLOGIST'S opinion. "At the time of the killing, Suzanne was impaired emotionally and unable to control her actions. Thus, she was unable to harbor premeditation or deliberation."

The DEFENSE rests.

The DA has two rebuttal witnesses. The first rebuttal witness, a psychologist hired to render an opinion of Suzanne Temple's mental condition, testifies that he reviewed the DEFENSE PSYCHOLOGIST'S test results and subsequent report and disagrees with her findings. "These tests merely show a 'snap shot' of an individual at the time of the testing, an individual who had been arrested and charged with murder."

The DA calls Alex Temple's father. This second rebuttal witness testifies that his son was happy with his marriage and, as he recalls, "always put Suzanne on a pedestal."

The DEFENSE has no other witnesses.

Outside the presence of the JURY, the JUDGE asks for arguments concerning the EXHIBITS being allowed into evidence. Neither attorney challenges the other. The exhibits are entered into evidence.

The attorneys provide closing arguments. The JUDGE instructs the JURY. Deliberation starts a week after the first witness was presented.

The JURY consists of eight women and four men. They notify the JUDGE several times over the next couple of days that they are deadlocked, but each time he sends them back into the JURY room to deliberate and reach a verdict. The last notification convinces the JUDGE that the JURY is hopelessly deadlocked.

The JURY breakdown is two for first degree murder—murder committed with deliberately premeditated malice aforethought (Black's Law Dictionary), eight for second degree murder—the unlawful taking of human life with malice, but without the other aggravating elements of first degree murder (Black's Law Dictionary) and two for voluntary manslaughter—manslaughter committed voluntarily upon a sudden heat of passions; as if, upon a sudden quarrel, two persons fight, and one of them kills the other. It is the unlawful taking of human life without malice and under circumstances falling short of willful, premeditated or deliberate intent to kill and approaching too near thereto to be justifiable homicide (Black's Law Dictionary).

The JUDGE declares a mistrial.

Name _____          Date _____

## QUESTIONS - CHAPTER FIVE

1.  You lost or misplaced the cassette tape of Suzanne Temple's confession. What do you attribute this error to?

2.  How did your mishandling of the taped confession affect court procedures?

3.  Define the term "stipulation."

Name _____          Date _____

## QUESTIONS - CHAPTER 5 CONTINUED

4. Why was the testing of the blood evidence important even though it was obviously Alex Temples?

5. What is meant by the term "laying foundation?"

6. How are police witnesses able to identify evidence items when they collected or analyzed the evidence over a year ago?

Name _____         Date _____

## QUESTIONS - CHAPTER 5 CONTINUED

7.  On cross-examination by the defense, the attorney has attempted to discredit you through personal attacks. Why do you feel she is doing this?

8.  Explain the chain of custody associated with the GSR test of Alex Temple.

9.  Explain the chain of custody associated with the bullet, casings and gun evidence.

Name _____          Date _____

## QUESTIONS - CHAPTER 5 CONTINUED

10. What are the common signs of death by cyanide poisoning?

11. Explain the chain of custody associated with the testing of blood for cyanide poisoning.

12. The cyanide expert testified that there was no trace of cyanide in Alex Temple's blood. How do you account for this?

Name _____          Date _____

## QUESTIONS - CHAPTER 5 CONTINUED

13. The book, *Deadly Doses,* seemed to be great evidence for the DA. How did the defense counter this evidence?

14. The defense used a psychologist to mitigate Suzanne's behavior. What was the psychologist's opinion of why Suzanne killed her husband?

15. How did the DA counter the psychologist's opinion?

*Chapter 6*

# Second and Third Trials

Six months have lapsed until the DA prepares to retry Suzanne Temple. In response to the notice of a second trial, the DEFENSE ATTORNEY files a motion to suppress the confession, the gun, the bullets and casings.

This is known as a 1538.5 motion where a hearing is scheduled in front of a JUDGE to determine the legality of the officers' actions upon retrieving evidence. The attorneys will submit *briefs* to the court prior to the hearing to explain their positions as to the officers' actions. If the JUDGE feels that the officers obtained the evidence illegally, then suppression of that evidence will be granted.

Subsequently, the DA invites you to join him in the courthouse cafeteria to confer about the motion. There, he orders two coffees and, since he is not a donut lover like you, two squares of corn bread with extra butter.

He has his wallet out and tells you that he'll pick up the tab. So, even though your taste buds are salivating for those chocolate things with holes in the middle that are stacked on the counter by the cash register, you force a smile and say thanks.

Priorities taken care of, the two of you find a table and sit down. The DA pulls out his yellow legal pad and refers, first, to the underlined word <u>confession</u>.

"Most certainly, the defendant's confession will be suppressed," he says. He points to the corn bread and encourages you to try some. Instead, you sip your coffee and, following your lead, he does the same before pointing out that even though Temple's statements were voluntary, she had asked for an attorney.

You agree. You know that even though she confirmed (at your prompting) in her own words (on tape) that she spoke to you voluntarily, this attempt to gloss over *Miranda* won't fly in court.

The JUDGE will likely suppress the defendant's statements from the point where she said, "I think that you're telling me, I need to see a lawyer. You don't believe what I am telling you. I'd like to have a lawyer."

The DA excuses himself a minute to get a refill on his coffee. On his return, he butters the second corn bread square, swallows a chunk and continues. He says he *could* argue that she wasn't in custody. *Could.* But the DA is too savvy to discount that you sent Temple to the police station, you ordered the GSR test on her, you spoke to her for several hours, and all are suggestive of a person being in custody by virtue of your authority.

"What about presenting her testimony from the first trial. She did confess to murdering her husband," you remind him.

"I don't know. Her testimony was pretty self-serving," he says.

A self-serving statement is an explanation of why you <u>had</u> to take the action. The purpose is to mitigate your actions in order to draw sympathy from the listener(s). In this case, the result would reduce accountability or forgive the action (killing).

"But, she did admit guilt."

"Yes, and her testimony was packed with excuses. I don't want the JURY to hear her excuses."

You remind the DA that the JURY will hear excuses through her psychologist's testimony. "So why not bring in Temple's testimony?"

The DA agrees to keep an open-mind about the defendant's prior testimony and moves on to the gun, bullets and casings. He asks your thoughts regarding a possible motion to suppress that evidence.

You assure him that the defendant was not coerced, that she directed you to that evidence of her own volition, after she confessed to the murder, and so the evidence will not be suppressed.

There is no "fruit of the Poisonous Tree" associated with *Miranda* unless the statement was coerced. *Miranda* protects against self-incrimination, meaning the spoken words *"I DID IT."* *Miranda* does not protect against the finding of other witnesses or real evidence that was provided by the suspect to the police. Therefore, even though police violate a suspect's *Miranda* rights and find evidence based on the suspect's statements, the evidence has been obtained legally.

"We'll be on the defensive if you can't bring in her prior testimony. Temple will have the advantage if the JURY is not allowed to hear her confession. Also, the JURY will get confused if we don't connect the confession to her taking me to the bowling alley for the bullet and casings and then the freeway embankment for the gun."

"I don't think they'll be confused," the DA says.

You don't share his optimism, but you hope it rubs off on the JURY.

The JUDGE, the same distinguished white-haired JUDGE who presided over the first trial, is back on the bench again. He remembers you and, after acknowledging the two attorneys, nods in your direction. As is his habit, the JUDGE prepares to listen to the tedius pretrial motions by supporting his face with his left palm.

The DEFENSE, in an interesting move, requests that the JURY hear Suzanne's statements from the interrogation, but only up to her request for an attorney. As rehearsed, the DA fights this request. He counters that Temple should testify if the request is granted.

Prior to the request for an attorney, Suzanne denied involvement in killing her husband. Suzanne was a good actor. She sounded very convincing and the recording picked up her sincerity. However, this act didn't move you because of the evidence you had implicating her.

"Your honor," the DEFENSE reminds the JUDGE, "my client cannot be forced to testify."

The JUDGE notes that when you violated Temple's right to an attorney, you violated her *Miranda* rights. He rules for the DEFENSE. Her confession after the violation, he says, will be suppressed. *Miranda v. Arizona* (1966) 384 U.S. 431-444.

The ruling regarding the gun, bullet and casings, however, is taken under submission and subsequently favors the State. The mindful JUDGE rules that Temple's statements made regarding that evidence after the *Miranda* violation were voluntary and that the *Miranda* violation does not affect your recovery of the gun, bullet and casings. There is no "fruit of the poisonous tree." *Elstad v. Oregon (1985) 470 U.S. 298.*

The last ruling favors the State as well; the DA can use Temple's prior testimony from the first trial. This is an exception to the hearsay rule.

Using the DA's yellow pad, you question what he plans to do about Temple's prior testimony.

Writing back, the DA tells you that he is not going to use it. "Too self-serving."

"No way to get around it, huh?"

Thinking, the DA scans your words, rubs his eyes with the palm of his hands and shakes his head.

"A waste of time," he writes.

Six men and six women make up the second JURY. Witness testimony extends over several days. The neighbors' memories are as sharp as at the first trial. The experts testify well.

The DA walks you hand-in-hand through the recovery of the gun evidence. Still, you sense the JURY is confused with the mismatched sequence of events: Temple is taken to the police station; Temple is given a GSR test; then, Temple takes you to the bowling alley and freeway embankment. Your testimony without the confession loses some of its bite. You hope, however, that in piecing your testimony together, they fill in the obvious gap

between the GSR test and police car ride with Temple to recover the murder weapon—
**Temple's confession to murder**.

> Unfortunately, the JURY's analytical reasoning may also include the following
> questions: If Temple confessed to the detective, why weren't we told? What
> did the detective do wrong? Indeed, the detective's professionalism and legal
> tactics are always uppermost in the JURY's mind.

As expected, Temple does not testify. Instead, the defendant's psychologist testifies.
Her testimony is thought provoking as is the cyanide expert's testimony.

A week later the JURY foreman advises the JUDGE of a possible hung jury—they
have been unable to agree on a verdict.

The JUDGE instructs the JURY to deliberate again.

They remain deadlocked: one JURY member votes for first degree murder, five for
second degree murder and six for voluntary manslaughter.

The JUDGE has no recourse; he declares a mistrial.

A new JUDGE has been selected to preside over the third trial. You have previously
appeared before her and in your mind you recall, for some reason, her striking blue eyes
and red lip color.

Today, four months after the conclusion of the second trial, she sits on the bench
listening to the DEFENSE attorney argue on behalf of the defendant. Against her black
robe, the JUDGE'S eyes are as intensely blue as you had remembered. Her silver hair is
cropped neatly above her ear lobes and her demeanor, as was evident to you before,
leaves no doubt that the courtroom is hers.

Indeed, this morning, after a speedy pretrial motion, she moves to suppress Temple's
taped confession. The DEFENSE further seeks to preclude all allegations of cyanide
poisoning. She argues for the following special JURY instruction:

"It should be presumed that the urine, had it been available, would have shown the
absence of cyanide."

The argument was based on the following points:

The coroner's lab was served with a court order for a urine split in order for the
defense to test for the presence of a cyanide metabolic, a method of cross-checking the
accuracy of the blood test. Subsequently, however, the DEFENSE discovered that the lab
destroyed all of the evidence it was holding in connection with this case while litigation was
pending.

Unfortunately, the accuracy of the blood test cannot be verified in any other way than
with the urine. In addition, even though the PROSECUTION requested a cyanide test in

a timely manner, the results were not available for many months and, as a result, the DEFENSE'S request for a urine split was delayed.

Nonetheless, a retest of the blood showed no detectible level of cyanide.

The DEFENSE then argued the following Points and Authorities:

- Due process requires the prosecution's agents to preserve evidence when it has exculpatory value that is apparent before destruction and the evidence is of such a nature that the defendant is unable to obtain comparable evidence by other reasonable means.

The coroner's lab had the duty to preserve Alex Temple's urine since it could have supplied evidence to clear Suzanne Temple of allegations of poisoning her husband. Also, it was important to preserve this evidence since it was the only way to cross-check the blood results.

- In addition, due process imposes a duty on the part of the police to preserved evidence when the evidence has apparent exculpatory value. *People v. Stansbury* (1993) 4 Cal 4th 1017; 17 Rptr 2nd 174.

The DETECTIVE had the duty to make sure that the coroner's lab preserve Alex Temple's urine. Since the DETECTIVE failed to do this, the coroner's lab destroyed all evidence.

Per *Brown v. Municipal Court* (1978) 86 Cal App 3rd 357, 150 Cal Rptr 216, the appropriate remedy is to suppress any blood evidence for cyanide based on the unavailability of a urine sample to impeach the blood evidence.

And, per *People v. Zamora* (1980) 28 Cal 3d 88, 167 Cal Rptr 573, an appropriate remedy may be for a JURY instruction advising the JURY that such urine test would have shown evidence to dispute the existence of cyanide in the victim's blood.

The DA argued that internal procedures caused the coroner's lab to inadvertently destroy Alex Temple's blood and urine samples. It was not the intent of the coroner's office to maliciously or wilfully deprive the DEFENSE of an alternative testing procedure. In addition, the DA argued that the DETECTIVE never requested that the blood and urine samples be destroyed.

The JUDGE brushes her bangs away from her forehead, looks down at the notes before her and closes her eyes momentarily. You and the attorneys wait. Looking up at both attorneys, the JUDGE advises that she rules for the DEFENSE—no reference to cyanide.

The DA and DEFENSE follow the same trial procedure as the previous trials with the exception of Suzanne's confession and the cyanide evidence.

Unquestionably, the case was weakened. Not yet defeated, the DA relied on the NEIGHBORS' statements and Suzanne's admission regarding the gun and bullet evidence. He tries to convince the JURY that Suzanne shot her husband in the head upstairs, then stalked him downstairs and shot him in the back. These are aggravating circumstances and proof that the murder was premeditated and deliberate.

What seemed to be a "slam-dunk" first degree murder case is in jeopardy. "What else could I have done," you think to yourself. It suddenly comes to you. I should have found the bullet fragment from the head shot. If it was found downstairs, then there would be no doubt of a premeditated murder—Alex was lying down, probably passed out when Suzanne shot him. Too late. Maybe she did shoot him in the head upstairs.

"What else," you wonder. The coroner's policy of destroying evidence after a year is etched into your mind. "I wish I would have known about this policy. Someone should make detectives aware of this." You make a mental note to distribute a memorandum to all the detectives advising them about the coroner's evidence destroying policy.

The DEFENSE again relies on the PSYCHOLOGIST to convince the JURY that mitigating factors prevailed, that the defendant's husband had mentally abused her.

The JURY, consisting of nine men and three women deliberated for several days but was unable to reach a verdict. Though the jurors exonerated Suzanne Temple of first degree murder, three voted for second degree murder and nine for voluntary manslaughter. The DEFENSE and her client are elated; you and the DA are numb. A third hung-jury.

The JUDGE declares a mistrial.

Name _____          Date _____

# QUESTION - CHAPTER 6

1.  The DA tells you that Suzanne Temple was *in-custody* at the time of her interrogation. What factors did he rely on?

2.  You disagree with the DA's assessment of Suzanne Temple's prior testimony as being self-serving. Explain.

3.  The DEFENSE wants the jury to hear Temple's statement to you until the point when she asked for an attorney. Why?

Name _____          Date _____

## QUESTIONS - CHAPTER 6 CONTINUED

4.  You have asked the coroner's office to test the victim's blood sample for poison. Should the victim's urine have also been tested? Explain.

5.  Unfortunately, the coroner's office disposed of Alex Temple's urine sample before it could be tested for cyanide, so possible corroboration of body fluid findings is not possible. How could positive urine findings have enhanced the prosecution's case?

6.  Would negative urine findings have had as large an impact as positive urine findings? Explain.

Name _____          Date _____

## QUESTIONS - CHAPTER 6 CONTINUED

7. Per *Brown v. Municipal Court*, what is a remedy for failing to keep Alex Temple's urine sample for testing?

8. As the JUDGE passes down her ruling regarding the cyanide suppression, you reevaluate what you could have done regarding the bullet evidence at the crime scene. Explain what could you have done, and how this could have *possibly* enhanced the case against Suzanne Temple.

# Afterword

Suzanne Temple's privately retained attorney allowed a few days to pass, then wrote the first of many letters that expressed her dissatisfaction with the District Attorney's office.

Pressured politically, the DA announces emotionally to his colleagues and to you that "If I have to, I'll find time in my busy schedule to try this case twice a year for the rest of my life."

Trying Temple again is not necessary. A month later, you and the DA take your usual places in the courtroom and listen to Temple plead guilty to voluntary manslaughter. This translates into 11 maximum years plus five years enhancement for the use of the gun. (A Judge has the authority to enhance the sentence by one, three or five years for gun use, and this JUDGE, the last JUDGE to try the defendant, chose to penalize the defendant with the maximum sentence.)

In total, the defendant, Suzanne Temple, receives a 16 year sentence for murdering her husband, Alex Temple (of which she will probably only serve eight.)